PORTRAIT OF

CALIFORNIA

PORTRAIT OF
CALIFORNIA

Photography by

Dewitt Jones

Larry & Donna Ulrich

Kerry Drager

Gary Geiger

Text by

Judith Morgan

GRAPHIC ARTS CENTER PUBLISHING®

International Standard Book Number 1-55868-249-X
Library of Congress Catalog Number 95-82156
Photographs pages 1, 2, 6, 7, 12, 15, 17, 20-21, 23, 24-25, 30, 40, 40-41, 47,
55, 57, 60, 60-61, 70, 72, 72-73, 74, 76, 77, 79, 80 © MCMXCV by Dewitt Jones
Photographs Front Cover, pages 8-9, 10, 19, 22, 34, 35, 36, 37, 38, 39, 42, 43, 44-45,
46, 48, 54, 56, 58, 59, 64, 65, 66, 67, 68-69, 71 © MCMXCV by Larry Ulrich
Photographs Back Cover, pages 26, 27, 28-29, 31, 32,
33, 62, 63, 75, 78 © MCMXCV by Kerry Drager
Photographs pages 49, 52-53 © MCMXCV by Gary Geiger
Photographs pages 50, 51 © MCMXCV by Monterey Bay Aquarium
Text © MCMLXXXIX by Graphic Arts Center Publishing®

President • Charles M. Hopkins
Editor-in-Chief • Douglas A. Pfeiffer
Managing Editor • Jean Andrews
Photo Editor • Diana S. Eilers
Production Manager • Richard L. Owsiany
Cartography • Tom Patterson and Manoa Mapworks
Book Manufacturing • Lincoln & Allen
Printed and bound in the United States of America

Front Cover: Sunlight strikes the rugged cliffs overlooking Bolinas Beach, as the early evening lights of San Francisco glow in the distance. *Half Title Page and Back Cover:* The California poppy, the state flower, flourishes throughout the state. *Frontispiece:* A rainbow graces the pool at the foot of Yosemite Falls.

CALIFORNIA

OREGON

Smith River
Crescent City

KLAMATH
MTNS

REDWOOD
NATL PARK

Trinidad Hbr

Eureka

Mendocino

Mendocino

Ukiah

Pt Arena

KLAMATH
NWR

Goose L.

CLEAR LAKE
NWR

LAVA BEDS
NATL MON

Alturus

MODOC NWR

NEVADA

CASCADE RANGE

TRINITY
ALPS

Weed
Mt. Shasta

Mt Shasta
x 14,162'

WHISKEYTOWN-
SHASTA-TRINITY
NATL REC AREA

Shasta L.

Redding

Eagle L.

LASSEN
VOLCANIC
NATL PARK

Lassen Pk
10,457' x

Susanville

Red Bluff

Thompson Pk
x 9002'

SACRAMENTO VALLEY

SIERRA

COAST RANGES

Eel River

Chico
Paradise
L. Oroville
Oroville

SACRAMENTO
NWR
DELEVAN
NWR

Marysville
SUTTER
NWR

Feather River

Yuba City

Donner Pass
7239'

Donner L.

South Lake Tahoe

Yuba River

Pt Reyes

FORT ROSS SP

Healdsburg
St Helena

Santa Rosa
Sonoma
Napa
Vacaville

SACRAMENTO

Placerville

American River

Lake Tahoe

NEVADA

Sonora Pass
9628'
Devils Gate
7519'

POINT REYES
NATL SEASHORE

Richmond
Bolinas
San Rafael

Vallejo
Berkeley

Lodi

Mokelumne River

Columbia

Pettit Pk
10,788' x

Tioga Pass
9941'

Mono L.

San Francisco Bay

Oakland

Stockton

YOSEMITE
NATL PARK

SAN FRANCISCO

AÑO NUEVO SR

Hayward

Modesto

Mammoth
Lakes

White Mtn Pk
x 14,246

Half Moon Bay

Livermore
Fremont
Palo Alto

San Jose

El Portal

DEVILS
POSTPILE
NATL MON

BRISTLECONE
PINE SP

Bishop

Santa Cruz

DIABLO
RANGE

SAN LUIS NWR
Merced
MERCED NWR

N Palisade
x 14,242

Big Pine

Monterey Bay

California Aqueduct

Finger Pk
x 12,404' Mt Pinchot
x 13,495'

SAN JOAQUIN VALLEY

KINGS CANYON
NATL PARK

Monterey
Carmel

Salinas

PINNACLES
NATL MON

Fresno

Mt Brewer
x 13,570'

DEATH VALLEY

Big Sur

Salinas River

San Joaquin River

Kings River

SEQUOIA
NATL PARK

Mt Whitney
x 14,494'
x 13,802' Mt Kaweah

Owens L.

Towne Pass
4956'

NATL MON

SAN ANDREAS FAULT

Coalinga

Visalia

Telescope Pk
x 11,049'

San Simeon

HEARST
CASTLE

Tulare L.

PIXLEY NWR

Kern River

China L.

KERN NWR

Los Angeles Aqueduct

Morro Bay

San Luis Obispo

Pismo Beach

Bueno
Vista L.

Taft

Carrizo Plain

Bakersfield

MOJAVE

Soda L.

DESERT

Santa Maria

Lompoc

Solvang

Condor
Refuge

Edwards

Lancaster

Barstow

Needles

L HAVASU NWR

Pt Conception

Santa Barbara

Ventura

SAN GABRIEL
MTNS

Victorville

SAN BERNARDINO
MTNS

Oxnard

LOS ANGELES

Pasadena

San Bernardino

Mojave River

Aqueduct

San Miguel I

Santa Barbara Channel

Beverly Hills
Glendale

DISNEYLAND

JOSHUA TREE
NATL MON

Blythe

CHANNEL ISLANDS
NATL PARK

Santa Cruz I

Santa Rosa I

Santa Monica
Santa Monica Bay

Anaheim

Long Beach
Balboa

Santa Ana

Palm Springs

Colorado River

San Pedro Channel

San Catalina I

Gulf of
Santa Catalina

ANZA-
BORREGO
DESERT SP

Salton Sea

SALTON SEA
NWR
Brawley

IMPERIAL NWR

San Nicholas I

Oceanside

Escondido

CHOCOLATE MTNS

San Clemente I

San Diego

CABRILLO NATL MON

Chula Vista

Calexico
Mexicali

IMPERIAL VALLEY

Yuma

Tijuana

MEXICO

BAJA
CALIFORNIA

Gulf of
California

Legend

Controlled Access Highways
Other Major Highways
National Wildlife Refuges
State Parks or Points of Interest
National Forest
National Park, Recreation Area, Seashore, or Monument
Approximate location of the San Andreas Fault

0   50   100   150 miles
0   50   100   150 kilometers

◁ The tallest trees in the world—the coastal redwoods or *Sequoia sempervirens*—tower more than three hundred feet high. △ Eagle Falls pounds into Lake Tahoe, North America's largest alpine lake. Lake Tahoe is twenty-two miles long and twelve miles wide, with an average depth of 989 feet. ▷ ▷ Monterey was for many years between 1775 and 1846 the provincial capital of Alta California.

△ Salmon and steelhead were once plentiful in biologically rich, pristine streams of the San Francisco Bay Area. Loss of habitat, due to environmental degradation, has reduced or eliminated these historic runs. Redwood Creek, one of the few streams that still supports these fish, drains the southwest slope of Mount Tamalpais, then flows through Muir Woods National Monument.

CALIFORNIA:

A STATE OF CELEBRATION

by Judith Morgan

OVERVIEW. Everything you have ever heard about California is probably true. Every roiling rumor can be confirmed somewhere along California's thousand-mile coast, or in the fastness of the Sierra Nevada, in the long farm valleys with year-round crops, or out in the lion-colored deserts. No exaggeration is too big for this most populous state, where the sun does shine an inordinate number of days each year.

California is an audacious showroom for the great triumphs and errors of nature. The world's tallest trees—the mighty redwoods—thrive near the wet north coast. The highest waterfall in the United States pounds into Yosemite Park. One county contains the highest and the lowest points of the contiguous forty-eight states—Mount Whitney and Death Valley. Between those two geologic monuments are stands of bristlecone pines, the oldest living things on earth.

Alaska and Texas are both larger than California, but neither has such diversity of climate and terrain. California stretches from the border of evergreen Oregon to the frontier of Mexico. The same latitudes along the eastern shore of the United States would reach from Cape Cod to Savannah, and touch eleven states.

With so much land, there is room to spread out, although Californians generally don't. Most of them crowd near the coast in joyful noise, like guests at a cocktail party. They lead fast-paced lives in cities held together by freeways. They drive miles to work and more miles to play.

Multiple images of California flash around the world, gleaned from Hollywood films or a bleep on the evening news. Pop songs and postcards spread cheery words about Disneyland and mission bells, space ships and cable cars, beaches and bikinis. There is truth, though not the whole truth, to such images. They flourish in the minds of the millions of people for whom California fills a need. Like a gorgeous, willful child, California stirs up feelings of admiration, amusement, and envy. You can love California's idiosyncrasies, or laugh at them, or both. Californians do.

After all, it was the rumors of sudden wealth in the foothills and streams east of Sacramento that set off the Gold Rush, just a century and a half ago. That boisterous migration launched the California legend of youth, optimism, and vigor. Other amazing tales have come true rapidly enough to bolster the magic of the name. The natural richness of California yielded gee-whiz stories about exotic agriculture and backyard bonanzas. Vast deposits of oil were discovered under Los Angeles in the 1920s, and, as if on cue, a gusher came in on the campus of the Beverly Hills High School. The movie industry fueled such legends, which fueled more movies.

A California style evolved—with casual dress, home-grown wines, barbecues, car worship, sun worship, an absorption with health, a madcap mobility, and always an eye on tomorrow. The world is accustomed to California as a source of fad and innovation. From miracle-spawning laboratories on its high-tech campuses to back-alley workshops where sleeker surfboards are designed, there's a mood of "Why not?"

In the race toward the future, orange groves have given ground for instant cities, and foothills have been flattened into malls. Airports and freeways and cul-de-sacs of suburbia have pushed tongues of concrete toward beach and forest. Still, the land prevails. Amid a rubble of false starts, Californians have established the capacity to rise up and reform, to turn whims into law, to set off in new directions to preserve the pristine. They lobby fiercely for earth, sky, and sea; for mountains, shore, and desert; for creatures large and small and sometimes human. Californians explore their state with pride, celebrating its majesty. They hug trees, stalk trout, and gaze at the patterns of fleeting fog. They treasure hideaways where calm can be replenished and spirits find room to soar.

This book is about such places: quiet forests and crystalline lakes, palm-ringed oases and sandy shores, myriad parks and snow-capped crests to which Californians look for recreation and reassurance. My particular refuge is a cabin in a Southern California forest of tall pine and fir and lilac, on a hillside where the seasons are more blatant than on the coast. Poplars and oaks and pistachio trees burn gold there in autumn; tulips and daffodils and iris sprout bravely in spring. It reminds me a little bit of a lot of places I have called home.

Each new wave of Californians speaks with affection of "back home," but most who move West stay. They put down roots in this rootless state and begin to establish traditions. No longer bound by old orders, they set out to make their mark. Aspirations are high. They believe anything is possible. Thus, myths of the Golden State are perpetuated because they are real. Or perhaps they are real because they are perpetuated.

SOUTHERN CALIFORNIA: THE COAST IS CLEAR. I awakened at the usual hour, but something was awry. No grid of shadows played on the wall from my bedroom shutters. Outside my room, gray fleets of clouds churned and tumbled across the Southern California sky, bringing the first rain in nine months. Gone were the customary blues and golds of this curious coastline—both a semi-tropical haven of nearly ideal climate and a desert rising up from the sea. Now rain glistened on the lacy leaves of a mellaleuca tree, a crafty companion that screens out urban traffic, yet preserves my peephole views of the sea as it sweeps in against the sandstone cliffs and wide beaches of San Diego.

The first rainstorm of winter transforms the coast. Sweet smells off the Pacific Ocean mix with jasmine and sage. Under a pearly dome, Southern California shows kinship to a longer settled world. Images of scudding clouds above the shores of England buffet the mind. Yet here the rain is a curiosity: it enchants children in search of a puddle to stomp, children who have never seen snow; it confuses freeway drivers, so spoiled by dry, fast lanes; it cleans the air, hoses the horizon, and perks up thirsty shrubs. It will not last.

Before I moved West, I was warned that this coast had grown crowded and noisy, wild with sun-bronzed surfers and purple-haired crazies on roller skates whose territories were inviolate. I think of that on December mornings when I walk along the jutting cliffs above La Jolla Cove.

The coast can be noisy in August, of course, but in winter, the only sound is a thunderous rumble. I know it is just the clatter of rolling rocks on a beach that has been stripped of summer sands. The coast can be crowded in August, too. But now only two white-haired women in floppy hats are sharing a park bench and gesturing

toward the surf with their canes. "Have you seen a whale this season?" they ask.

Gray whales go by each winter, migrating from the Bering Sea to the lagoons of Baja California. Sightings are reason to cheer, but I have seen nothing yet. As I scan the horizon, a squadron of pelicans skims so close to the sheen of the sea that their beaks seem to trace their reflections. And surfers in black wet suits are bobbing far out on the swells. Or are those dolphins? In the glare, it is hard to be sure.

The California coast pushes on for twelve hundred miles between Mexico and the border of Oregon. But it is the two hundred miles of shore bordering Southern California that is the year-round playground, its parks and beaches and frothy waves the stuff of legend. Hang-gliders waft like butterflies above the sands. Kite-fliers race with the wind. Flame-tipped agave plants sprout beside craggy trails, and the frosted pink blooms of ice plant are scattered on the cliffs like Persian carpets. While they seem like props from movie sets, palm trees are real and plentiful, as are twisted junipers and cypress.

Four out of five Californians live within thirty miles of the coast; the less populous mountains and desert lie to the east. It is a miracle of the densely settled southern coast, with its glittering trappings of leisure and military might, that most of the shoreline remains accessible to everyone. Catamarans and windsurfers share San Diego's boot-shaped harbor with ferry boats and Navy air-craft carriers. Thousands of yachts are moored near their owners' front gates, from Coronado to Newport Beach to Marina del Rey. The Santa Monica beach has been popular for more than a century.

The neighboring enclave of Malibu offers seclusion to Hollywood celebrities. Venice, by contrast, is extroverted; its boardwalk is where people go to be discovered in a parade of muscle-bound bodies and carnival acts. The coast of Southern California evokes comparisons to the Riviera—until you plunge into the Pacific Ocean and feel how much colder it is than the Mediterranean.

Seasonal shifts are subtle. There is no classic spring or fall. In summer, the coast is the patio of the southwest, where residents of sweltering climates seek relief. In winter, the coast resumes its contemplative character, and you know it is December by the fiery bloom of poinsettia and the rare splash of morning rain.

VALLEYS OF WINE AND FOOD. Elsewhere in the world, wine-and-food societies gather in a ritual pursuit of gustatory pleasures. In the egalitarian state of California, the chase never ends. Three hundred food festivals celebrate home-grown produce and the bounties of land and sea. Thousands of Californians drive hundreds of miles to honor an eggplant or an onion. Forty festivals toast the state's wines.

Agriculture is California's leading industry, and grapes are big business. California produces three of every four bottles of wine that are drunk in America. There are wineries in forty-three of the state's fifty-eight counties. Wine talk is no longer snobby. Tastings turn into charity fund-raisers. Swap-meets of vintage wines draw large crowds. Hospitals routinely offer wine as a mealtime beverage. Students earn advanced degrees in viniculture from the University of California, Davis.

Wine making was introduced in California by Franciscan fathers during their mission-building spree in the late 1700s. It came of age in 1857 when Agoston Haraszthy, a Hungarian emigrant, planted European vines in Sonoma County. The best-known region is the elegant Napa Valley, less than fifty miles from San Francisco, where more than 185 vintners produce premium wines. Autumn in the Napa Valley is a heady time of golden sunsets and ripe, sweet air as vines are picked clean for the crush. A lavender haze hangs over plaited vineyards and the pitched roofs of frame houses that seem part of another time. This is a gentle land of wrap-around porches and lace curtains, of farm lanes and rolling hills. The country restaurants are as charming as those of Burgundy or Provence. The pace of life is set by the growing season.

One September evening in St. Helena, I sipped a glass of Sauvignon Blanc and listened to a young innkeeper, a refugee from San Francisco, talk of the rhythm of the land: "I love the sing-song of the grape pickers in the vineyards at daybreak," she said in a voice wreathed in calm. "And later in the morning, on the roads through town, there's the rumble of the gondola trucks, heavy with grapes from the harvest. Pretty soon you hear this springy sound—boing, boing, boing—and you know they're empty and heading back to the vineyards."

Napa and the neighboring counties—Lake, Sonoma, and Mendocino—enjoy long, sunny seasons and cool fog covers of classic wine zones.

But the giants in grape production are in the Great Central Valley, an enormous, pan-flat trough as large as Vermont and New Hampshire combined. The valley extends more than 450 miles from Redding in the north to beyond Bakersfield in the south, almost half the length of the state. Its landscape is marked by monotony: roads straight as furrows; canals as straight as roads; and scattered, look-alike towns. The Great Central Valley contains a sixth of all irrigated land in the United States. The hot sun and fertile soil bring an abundance and variety of produce as boggling as the scenery is lackluster.

The largest winery in America, the family-owned empire of Ernest and Julio Gallo, is based in Modesto. This aptly-named community is perhaps best known as the home of George Lucas and as the inspiration for his film, "American Graffiti." It also is the home of the largest almond factory in the world, a place where plant tours give motorists a reason to slow down.

The heart of the raisin kingdom—those grapes grown dry and wrinkled—lies to the south, between Fresno and Selma. Packing sheds glint in the sun. The valley is a natural hot-house for a multitude of vegetables, fruits, and nuts: asparagus, tomatoes, potatoes, pears, peaches, plums, prunes, oranges, lemons, grapes, apricots, raisins, nectarines, olives, walnuts, almonds.

In contrast, smaller farm pockets in other California valleys go for the exotic. Along the winding backroads of Sonoma County are stands that sell designer mushrooms, celadon cabbages, and red Russian kale. Sebastopol specializes in Gravenstein apples and delicate berries. Despite urban growth, San Diego County still has acres in avocados and kiwi fruit. Lush Santa Clara Valley south of San Francisco Bay is the world's leading producer of prunes.

In Salinas Valley, inland from the coast at Monterey, the lettuce crop is augmented by cauliflower, celery, onions, carrots, broccoli, and garbanzo beans. Although it is proud to be the birthplace of John Steinbeck, Salinas also boasts of being the Salad Bowl of the World. The neighboring community of Castroville produces virtually all of the artichokes grown in the nation. Gilroy claims world rank for its garlic, which is honored with a blow-out festival in July. Pungent recipes are cooked at sidewalk stands. Garlic-flavored candy is a best-seller.

Even more amazing is what sprouts in the searing high desert called Mojave. Through the wonder of irrigation, the desert is host to almond orchards and watermelons. To the south, the Imperial Valley, with its teetering dunes and stultifying heat, brings in multiple crops of lettuce and cantaloupes. They seem to ripen in a blink, thanks to the nearby

Colorado River and the arteries of the All-American canal. In Coachella Valley, southeast of Palm Springs, royal oases of dark palm groves are hung with exotic bouquets of dates — plump medjools and deglet noors. Grapes and grapefruits also thrive.

Fragrant orange trees, which launched those agricultural legends and real estate booms a century ago, still can be found within the boundaries of the Southern California cities they helped to build: Riverside, San Bernardino, Pasadena, Santa Ana, Redlands, Pomona, and the city of Orange. But most of the fabled groves have given way to residential subdivisions, industrial parks, and university campuses.

It is a peculiar state of affairs when more people turn out for a whiff of garlic than for orange blossoms. Peculiar, California, and potent.

THE REDWOOD NORTH. North of the Golden Gate, the coast grows somber, the sun is duller than in the south, the sea more demanding. Salt winds skew pines and cypresses into gaunt silhouettes. The San Andreas Fault follows the coast conspicuously, showing its path in ominous sinks and scarps. Remnants of redwood forests haunt the coastal ridges as far south as Santa Cruz and Monterey. But the virgin groves are far to the north. Here, untouched, are the tallest of trees, the noble giants that bring braggarts to silence.

For more than four hundred miles stretching from San Francisco's Golden Gate to the border of Oregon, this is a sparsely settled coast with wild meadows and rangeland that is marked by weathered rail fences—a place of egret preserves and sheer headlands and national seashores. It is a coast that has not shared in the extravagant march of California. It is also supremely beautiful.

Only four towns have grown to more than two thousand; the largest is Eureka, with a population of just over twenty-four thousand. Isolated by history, foul weather, and a precipitous shoreline, it is a land of grit and gumption, loggers and fishermen, idealists and loners and sheep. Beaches are wracked with driftwood. Seastacks rise from the surf like drunken greeters. Fog is a factor in daily life, routinely blotting out the other side of the road and playing havoc with airline schedules.

It is also a land of ghosts. For the Spanish, this was the far north, a land mistrusted; for the Czarist Russians, it was a momentary southern outpost, a land unfulfilling. Tales here are of treacherous reefs, shipwrecks, and monster waves, such as one that struck a bluff in 1913 and shot over the Trinidad

Head Light. The Coast Guard logs show that the light, then as now, was 196 feet above mean low tide. In the spring of 1964, Crescent City was hit by seismic sea waves triggered by the Good Friday Earthquake centered near Anchorage, Alaska. The worst wave was thirty feet high and moving at five hundred miles an hour when it left Anchorage to crash into the harbor at Crescent City. Eleven people died.

Even the north coast rivers, with their abrupt names—Elk, Eel, Mad, Noyo—can turn violent. For most of the year they are subdued streams, but their banks are scarred with reminders of their force. In the fall of 1964, Indian women warned of a hard winter. Tiny green frogs appeared high in the trees as they had before heavy floods in other years. The snows fell early. In December, the rains began and pounded for six days. At Alderpoint, the Eel River rose more than ninety feet, washing mountains of logs from lumberyards to form miles-wide jams out at sea. The towns of Klamath and Pepperwood were destroyed. Disasters, heroism, and survival—when North Coasters tell these heart-stopping tales they look proud.

Holds on this wave-scoured coast have always been tenuous. In 1812, officers of the Russian American Fur Company in Alaska established an outpost on the Sonoma coast to serve as a base for the hunting of sea otters and a place to raise foodstuffs for the Alaskan operation. The name, Fort Ross, was from an archaic word for Russia. Theirs was the first flag to fly on this coast, their Orthodox chapel the first church. The Russians planted apple orchards, wheat, and sloeberries to flavor their vodka. They cut redwood trees and built a stockade. But the land wore thin, and their slaughter of sea otters all but exterminated the herds. In 1841 the Russians left Alaska and sold their California property. The buyer was John Augustus Sutter, the wily Swiss who owned the mill where gold was discovered seven years later.

The true patriarchs of the north are the *Sequoia sempervirens*, redwoods that reach up to 350 feet, with trunks twenty feet in diameter. The Sierra redwoods, which are found in Sequoia and Kings Canyon National Parks, have greater girth and age but are not as tall. Redwoods are imperturbable—epic in their indifference to fire, parasites, and disease. Millions of board feet of redwood were shipped south during the last century to build San Francisco's hilltop mansions and docks and to provide siding and shingles for roofs around the world. More than one hundred thousand acres of the massive trees have been preserved in Redwood National Park, which flanks Highway 101 in Humboldt and Del Norte

Counties. Loggers and environmentalists still argue whether that is too much or not enough.

Early one morning near the Smith River, I struggled to keep pace with John Green, a sixty-six-year-old Indian logger who was born on this coast. He bounded up the steep forest road with his tools slung over his shoulder—a fifty-four-inch power saw, an iron knockout bar, and an ax. All was silent except for the creak of some great limb twenty stories above. I had not realized that one man could take a redwood, or would even try.

"We'll fell a good-size one," he said, his voice as gentle as a child's. The tree was about seven feet thick and more than two hundred feet tall, rising a hundred feet before its first branches appeared. Without a word, he revved up his saw and drove it into the tree. Red sawdust spurted out like dried flecks of blood and buried his boots. The musty smells of bark and soil hung in the air. As he walked around the giant, making ritual slashes, a tractor came over the rise and began to clear a bed as long as the tree was high. "Those mounds of earth keep the tree from shattering when it hits," John explained.

With his bar, he knocked out a slab of trunk. Jacks went into the gap. He moved to the other side and made the undercut, a deep wedge that left the center of the trunk as a hinge. Then his snarling saw fell quiet. "It's ready," he said. "Move back." Then he gave the warning bellow: ". . . berr!"

The tree shuddered, leaned, then hesitated. With a sharp crack, the trunk snapped. The tree gained speed, leaped outward, and finally struck its bed with thunderous force. John climbed up on the stump and studied the rings. "It's about 540 years," he said. "I thought it was older." I stood staring upward. The sky seemed empty.

I LEFT MY HEART IN YERBA BUENA. San Francisco rakes at the memory. The city is too bold and bawdy and beautiful to be confused with any other. All of us who go as tourists recount with pleasure what we have seen and tasted and smelled. Weren't we the first ones to clang downhill on that Powell Street cable car? Or to see the Golden Gate Bridge knocked out by a fist of fog? Had anyone else ever stumbled onto the morning serenity of tai chi at Portsmouth Square in Chinatown? Or watched the dawn break over Alcatraz?

I have never lived in San Francisco, and yet I seem to migrate there for special moments. The natives are tolerant of bedazzled strangers. They have been bedazzled, too. Perhaps they even envy us our stays, detached from the civic turmoils and the reality of urban nightmares.

On a spring break from college, I drank my first champagne in the spritzy city by the bay. In the gleaming Redwood Room of the Clift Hotel, I fell irrevocably in love. On that summer night when Barry Goldwater received the Republican Party's nomination for President of the United States, I received a jade engagement ring from a fellow reporter in the press gallery. That was at the old convention arena called the Cow Palace, clearly proving that any place in the realm of San Francisco can be touched by magic. San Francisco is a gracious host to both the revelers and the romantics, a city of grand opera and bitter-sweet trysts. The cool summers and mild winters of the peninsula attract visitors who come with a rich agenda and are seldom disappointed.

We outsiders wander the lanes off Grant Avenue in Chinatown and listen to the clack of mah-jongg tiles in endless unseen games. We hear the babble of Cantonese from the high windows of St. Mary's Chinese School, where Chinese-American youngsters are learning their ancestors' language. During the eight days of Chinese New Year, the cacophony bolts off the scale: thousands cheer the lion dancers and the Golden Dragon that snorts and careens through the streets to the din of gongs and drums and firecrackers. Chinatown is pagoda roofs, herbalists, and carts heaped with bok choy and snow peas. A gentle knock on the latched door of a Buddhist temple brings admittance to a sanctuary sweet with incense and offerings of red tangerines. A hundred restaurants are gathered in the twenty-four square blocks of Chinatown, and forty-three hundred in San Francisco. Tantalizing foods from far corners of the world have long been a hallmark of this city, which seems to have been born with taste.

Although the name San Francisco appeared on the sea charts of explorers as early as 1590, the site was first called Yerba Buena, for a lively anchorage of the 1830s. Yerba Buena, "good herb," was the name the Spanish had given to a fragrant creeper they found there. In 1847, just a year after statehood, the city was christened San Francisco. The first docks were built in that same year, and within months, the gold that would mold California was discovered inland at Sutter's Mill; and San Francisco became the target of fortune-seekers. In 1869, the city was linked with the eastern part of the United States by railroad. Italian families launched the fishing industry at Fisherman's Wharf. Soon, cable cars began clattering over the steep hills. When the cables were silenced for two years of overhaul in the 1980s, the city seemed estranged from itself and noticeably ill at ease.

The earthquake that tore San Francisco apart began at dawn of April 18, 1906. Walls crumbled, gas mains and water lines were ruptured. The fire that fed on this city of redwood timbers was finally halted by the dynamiting of buildings and homes, destroying all but a few traces of the city's nineteenth-century architecture. More than 450 people died. Survivors still gather each April at memorial breakfasts.

As the city was rebuilt, it grew tall and white, a cluster of towers atop noble hills, a city of big parks and small gardens, of narrow houses with bulging bay windows which were designed to accommodate the city's bountiful views. San Francisco is compact and vertical, as unlike Los Angeles as imagination will allow. It is a city that voted to suspend construction on downtown loop freeways, leaving a stub end that hangs near the grand old face of the Ferry Building on the Embarcadero. It is a city for walking.

San Francisco is European and Pacific and old California, a lovable sophisticate that smells of roses and fine chocolate, espresso coffee and sourdough bread. Its sounds are a concert of voices and tongues, of cable bells and basso foghorns that reverberate from the bay.

To me, those horns are not mournful, but celebratory, a fraternal call to friends on shore that it is curtain time, a moment to look up and savor the spectacle. I know of no other fog like the showy tufts that blow in from the Pacific and embrace the Golden Gate Bridge. Tugged by the heat and low pressure of inland valleys, the capricious fog shrouds one hill in gray, at the same time leaving the next crowned with gold.

On weekends, San Francisco is a jukebox of rattles and moans, laughter and street music. It is a splendid stage for impromptu performances. Nowhere do mimes seem more at home. The dramatic backdrop is the Golden Gate Bridge, whose towers seem to float between the city and the nubby, green hills of Marin County. Cruise ships and ferry boats and gleaming yachts cut through the mile-wide straits which were named the Golden Gate by explorer John C. Fremont, two years before gold was discovered.

A walk across the windswept bridge or a hike up a city hill inevitably makes me hungry. Fine food, after all, is at the heart of the San Francisco legend. In its presence, talk of lesser delights fades.

Not long ago, I had a birthday lunch at the Clift Hotel with another tourist, that grand old novelist, James Michener. We lingered long, talking of friends and travels, and I snapped his photograph. When I mailed the picture to the hotel manager, his response was pure San Francisco: "Although Mr. Michener looks great, I was not so pleased with the look of the fruit salad and have made some changes."

DESERTS OF LIFE AND DEATH. From the windows of a jet seven miles above the earth, Southern California deserts seem drab and empty. Like a rumpled rug, the dry land unrolls from Death Valley south through the immense Mojave to the lower and hotter Colorado Desert and Mexico. Railroad and freeway junction towns and military bases are scattered like spills of ashes among the natural rips and frays of this scorched and upturned land.

The Mojave Desert alone occupies one-sixth of California. It is a place of battered mountains and crusty basins, spiny Joshua trees and dry lake beds that become landing strips for secret aircraft and space missions. Coastal Californians tow their recreational vehicles to play on Mojave sands. Irrigated fields produce sweet melons. But those who look down from a jet seldom suspect such diversity. Perspective is blurred in this widest part of California. From the air, even Los Angeles looks manageable, lying to the west beyond the San Gabriel Mountains like a toy city of interlocking parts.

At the eastern horizon, the desert is interrupted by a wavy line as the Colorado River pushes southward toward Mexico. In this lowest desert there are flashes of color. The Salton Sea, thirty-five miles long and more than two hundred feet below sea level, glints like an opal in the sand. The golf courses of Palm Springs resorts link with the date groves of Indio to form a necklace of jade.

Most notorious of the California desert regions is Death Valley, a harsh wasteland 150 miles long that is littered with fearsome names taken from Dante and the devil. The lowest spot in the United States is there, on the salt flats of Badwater, 282 feet below sea level. If clouds do not intervene, and they rarely do in this desert, it is possible to look across eighty-five almost uninhabited miles to Mount Whitney, which, at 14,494 feet, is the highest point in California. In summer, Death Valley is consistently the hottest place on earth. Its record temperature was set July 10, 1913—134 degrees Fahrenheit in the shade. In 1917, there were forty-three consecutive days of temperatures over 120 degrees. Death Valley is a long way from civilization, but worth the drive. Las Vegas is 140 crooked miles to the south and east. Across the Panamint Range to the west, it is almost that far to Lone Pine, the town nestled at the foot of Mount Whitney.

Death Valley is especially eerie at night. Lights dance across the black hole of the valley floor from thirty to forty miles away but never seem to get closer. Of course they are cars, I tell myself, but where do they go? One of the stranger spectacles is a sudden golden glow suspended in the dark, an apparition like a sultan's palace in the Sahara. It turns out to be the lights of the Furnace Creek Inn, the toast of winter, an eccentric lodge built on a desert shelf in 1927. Inside, the fantasy continues; grotto pools and potted palms echo another era. Furnace Creek attracts an intriguing crowd, conservative Pasadenans who honeymooned there half a century ago and other couples who just met at Nevada gaming tables. Northwesterners come to escape winter rains. Fans of mystery films come in search of the ghost of Peter Lorre.

Modern Californians enjoy challenging Death Valley. In their air-conditioned vans and motor homes, they roll in for midsummer encampments. Motorcyclists and horseback riders take to its trails; hikers and joggers test their endurance against the elements.

A less extreme desert area, and perhaps my favorite, is Anza-Borrego Desert State Park, encompassing half a million acres on the east side of San Diego County. This is where I was first introduced to the desert by a mutual friend, a retired doctor who had spent years exploring its flinty canyons and grape-colored mounds. As a confirmed mountain person, I had never met a desert I liked, and he knew it.

One March day he took me touring in his Jeep, asking only that I be quiet and be fair. We jiggled past the crossroads of Ocotillo Wells and then turned sharply off into the sand. "The Gulf of California came up past here about fifteen million years ago," he said. "A few million years later a fresh water lake buried this desert." I looked at him, assuming it was a joke. He did not smile. The noon sun made the only waves in sight, little eddies that sizzled on the horizon. We drove on through sandy washes and past

windswept dunes. He stopped. "We'll walk from here," he said. "But beware of oyster shells." The spell of the desert began to take hold. I stretched out on the sand to gaze at tiny reefs of shell fossils. Through my camera lens, they were jagged mountains. Small became large and beautiful. The silence was as startling as the natural conundrum that my friend suggested. "Some of these fossils are of species that have only been found in the Atlantic Ocean," he said. "Think that over."

Before I could, he had found other minuscule miracles: wildflowers so small that I needed a magnifying glass to study their petals. Yet, in the millions, they formed a yellow stubble on the desert floor. At noon we shared a thermos of lemonade beside a venerable survivor, a lone palm that grows from a sandy crevice in the folds of badlands, miles from any other tree. Later, we saw the sharp toothmarks of desert foxes and coyotes and rabbits. We saw rounded sandstone concretions thrown up by nature, like pumpkins in a patch. Along the Fish Creek Wash, deep within the ash-white branches of a smoke tree, we found a newly hatched thrush peering from its nest, its camouflage almost flawless as it awaited its mother's return. My friend had made his point. When I cross the California desert in a jet, I think of the tiny flecks of life in that rough carpet.

SIERRA NEVADA: HIGH AND MIGHTY. It is the spine of California, this mighty Sierra Nevada, a towering mountain range that gives symmetry to the land. And it is more—an almost spiritual source of strength and tradition, a wilderness shrine to which Californians retreat from crowded cities and steamy towns and freeways. The Sierra serves as the lofty common ground where the dissonant regional voices of north and south are quieted in awe, in shared history, in a mutual sense of proprietorship.

And no wonder. The Sierra Nevada exceeds even the Rockies in height and length, and almost matches the combined Swiss, French, and Italian Alps in height and area. Like the Andes of South America, it is a bold link in the mountain chain that parallels the Pacific Coast from Cape Horn to the Aleutian Islands. It is home to Mount Whitney and other fourteen-thousand-foot peaks; it is also home to Lake Tahoe, a deep cup of crystalline water more than twenty miles long and ringed with forest. In its foothills, early settlers found gold. These days, the challenges lie on hiking trails and ski slopes and at the ends of fly-fishing lines. But one benevolence of the Sierra Nevada often goes overlooked. Its summits snag the prevailing westerlies off the Pacific and bring down moisture that relieves the California desert, builds the snowpack and fills water reservoirs to sustain the cities of the urban coast.

This range rises near volcanic Lassen Peak in the north and stretches southward for 430 miles, curving in concert with the coastline to the outer fringe of Los Angeles. For many Californians, it provides an eastern horizon; for the scattered desert settlements in its lee, its sheer escarpment is an even more dominant bulwark—a resting place for the eyes.

The heart of the Sierra Nevada is Yosemite National Park, a rock-ribbed wilderness filled with abundant reminders of the handholds that connect past and present. Within this park is Yosemite Valley, a magical bowl of searing light, dazzling rainbows, and moons that are fuller than dreams. My favorite approach to Yosemite Valley is through a tunnel in the mountains beyond the century-old resort of Wawona. Darkness stirs the imagination. The light at the end reveals a staggering view: El Capitan, a three-thousand-foot shaft of granite, storms up on the left; Bridalveil Fall, a wispy cascade, sparkles on the right. The flat face of Half Dome, nearly a mile wide, looms on the far horizon. Below is a meadow—a wild garden of pine and oak, of incense cedar and long-leaf fern—through which the clear Merced River flows. Beyond, Yosemite Falls drops 2,425 feet in three frothy stages, passing through a tangle of cataracts and pools before the final leap to the valley floor.

This is all snow melt, and May is its peak. By Labor Day the flow is reduced to a trickle. The golden walls have begun to dry, leaving only a shadow of lichen where the spray has been. This magnificent valley covers only seven square miles in a park that is the size of Rhode Island.

When it fills with the crowds of summer, it is time to escape to the higher country that John Muir so loved. Muir was the father of Yosemite Park, a naturalist and poet who pushed for preservation of national parkland. His spirit is still up there, reborn each summer with the opening of Yosemite's High Sierra camps whose names salute the morning: Sunrise, Glen Aulin, Merced, May Lake, Vogelsang. These tent camps are small, fanning out from the Tuolumne Meadows in a ragged circle accessible only on foot or by mule. While fifty thousand hikers and backpackers take out wilderness permits

each summer to walk these trails, only fifty mule riders can make the trip during each of the nine or ten weeks that the camps are open. From early July into September, the camps provide a key to the Sierra Nevada for those who love these peaks but not the challenge of backpacking their provisions. I am one of those people, fit with more dreams than stamina, loving my wilderness and hot breakfast, too.

For six days one August, I placed my trust in a sure-footed mule named Buttermilk, a kindly beast with coarse golden hair and eyes of liquid amber. We met at the stables at Tuolumne Meadows and traveled the Sierra Nevada together. Buttermilk held a steady gait, fording the icy streams, ambling through alpine meadows, and gingerly mounting rough granite stairs by the shores of glacial lakes. Each day after a picnic beneath skies of stained-glass blue, I gave Buttermilk an apple from my pack. Only once did she spurn the offer, her eyes avoiding mine, her ears turned forward. I crooned that it was okay. She refused to budge. Then I followed her gaze and saw the cinnamon bear with her cub. They crossed our path and lumbered to the far side of the stream. We followed parallel courses for much of an hour, smudges of gold in the brush.

In this hushed and ethereal world, the sound of cascading water is heard miles away. Forests of hemlocks and fragrant Jeffrey pines are so deeply carpeted that the cry of a magpie is startling. Deer graze unafraid in grassy glades. Meadow squirrels, called picket pins, stiffen on their haunches like tiny periscopes, and then zip back into their holes. The only light more compelling than the gilded pink of sunrise is the plum of alpenglow.

On our last night at the highest camp, the timberline perch of Vogelsang above ten thousand feet, the temperature fell into the 30s. Sheer winds rattled the tent flaps; blocks of cedar firewood snapped in our small stove. I pulled out a flashlight to read from the notes of John Muir. A century ago, he had written of the need for solitude, of the healing power of these blessed mountains "so compactly filled with God's beauty, no petty personal hope or experience has room to be." With a blanket around my shoulders, I ventured into a night of black velvet.

A light blinked far overhead, where a jet flew along one of the transcontinental paths between San Francisco and New York. It was a silent reminder that this was the twentieth century, a reminder that if I could be standing alone in that wilderness, depending on a golden mule to carry me out, the California legends of wonder and opportunity are not lost.

△ At Sunset Cliffs Park in Ocean Beach, several trails descend to the beaches, some accessible only at low tide. These sandstone concretions are at Osprey Point. ▷ ▷ Pleasure craft pack marinas near downtown San Diego. Boating is big in the boot-shaped harbor where U.S. Navy aircraft carriers home-port and America's Cup sailors train in a year-round temperate climate.

△ Cabrillo National Monument was named for the explorer who first landed at Point Loma. The Old Point Loma Lighthouse, shown here, was built in 1855, but because it was often obscured by fog, it was replaced in 1891 by a new lighthouse closer to San Diego Bay's entrance. ▷ Angular glass skyscrapers are softened by the Spanish architecture of the Santa Fe railway station in San Diego.

△ The bold flair and colorful tradition of Mexico's master muralists is carried on north of the border by Hispanic artists on such outdoor easels as this wall in San Diego.

◁ Westin Mission Hills Resort in Rancho Mirage offers bold land-
scaping. △ Many types of cacti thrive in a variety of ecosystems in
California's desert, including this barrel cactus on the flanks of the
Providence Mountains in the East Mojave National Scenic Area.
▷ ▷ Cholla cacti boast many names: Bigelow, teddybear, jumping.

△ Groves of date palms frame a hot-air balloon in Coachella Valley near Indio, not far from the Salton Sea. Dates are the thirstiest of all desert crops, but return the most value per acre. About 90 percent of the nation's date crop comes from this area. ▷ Desert Resorts Area events range from golf to polo to art and music fairs.

◁ Aguereberry Point is a feature along the Emigrant Canyon Road
in Death Valley National Park. △ Some say the spirits of Joshua
trees dance in the dark. Besides the wonderfully contorted trees,
Joshua Tree National Park offers great rock outcrops that have
become popular with climbers and sightseers.

△ San Juan Capistrano's East Corridor is just outside the Chapel, California's oldest building and the state's only remaining one used by Fray Junípero Serra. The Mission is also famous for the swallows that return each March 19 to the grounds. ▷ Western sycamore and coast prickly pear grow in Bell Canyon in Ronald W. Caspers Wilderness Park, in the foothills of the Santa Ana Mountains.

◁ Ochre seastars and purple urchins are exposed by a minus tide along the rocky shores of Channel Islands National Park. △ Avalon is the waterfront population center of Catalina Island. Reminiscent of a Mediterranean-style village, it is perched on a hill overlooking Avalon Bay. The Holly Hill House in the foreground and the Casino in the distance are part of the colorful history of Catalina Island.

△ Southern California coast's warm water and steady winds make it a sailors' paradise. Once busy commercial ports, Newport Bay and Balboa Island now overflow with pleasure craft and yachts.
▷ Each winter, western and ringed-billed gulls congregate near Pelican Point in Crystal Cove State Park, which protects three and one-quarter miles of coastline just south of Newport Bay.

◁ Spectacular fireworks gild the summer sky over the fluted turrets of Disneyland's Magic Kingdom, which has attracted more than 300 million visitors—from toddlers to foreign dignitaries—since it opened in 1955. △ On a clear night, when Southern California is working just right, you can see forever in the electrified glitz of Greater Los Angeles, a sprawl of ninety-four communities.

◁ The Malibu Pier, one of the original buildings in Malibu, was built in 1906 and 1907 to bring supplies in and out of the roadless area that is now Malibu. △ Rising out of the sand on San Miguel Island are forms of "fossil forests," or *caliche.* ▷ ▷ Called Queen of the Missions, the Santa Barbara Mission was built in 1786 by Franciscan friars to bring Christianity to the Chumash Indians.

◁ Rising 581 feet at the entrance to Morro Bay, Morro Rock is a nesting site for the endangered peregrine falcon. △ One man's fantasies are displayed with gusto at the castle built above San Simeon by publisher William Randolph Hearst. Greco-Roman pools and marble terraces glitter on 123 acres. The main house boasts thirty-eight bedrooms along with priceless tapestries.

△ Scenic Coast Highway 1 through Big Sur, completed in 1937, heads toward Bixby Creek Bridge. ▷ In the early 1900s, Cannery Row boomed with the business of canning sardines. Around 1950, when the sardines disappeared from the waters off Monterey, the canneries went out of business. These weathered, dilapidated relics are all that remain of the old canneries.

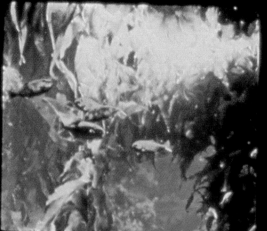

◁ Monterey Bay Aquarium includes this three-story-high exhibit—the tallest indoor aquarium exhibit in the world. △ Once hunted nearly to extinction, sea otters, like this one from Monterey Bay Aquarium, now occupy coastal waters from southern Big Sur to northern Monterey Bay. ▷ ▷ The sixteenth hole at Cypress Point Golf Course requires a drive off the tee over water.

△ The San Francisco-Oakland Bay Bridge links San Francisco with the East Bay cities and is the world's longest suspension span. From Yerba Buena Island, the winter sunset is directly over San Francisco's downtown skyline. ▷ A wreath of the famed San Francisco fog rolls in from the Pacific, passing the Sunset District, south of Golden Gate Park, on its billowy journey downtown.

◁ The Golden Gate Bridge, with its massive towers rising 746 feet above water level, is perhaps the most identifiable landmark on the California coast. △ San Francisco's bright burgundy cable cars, which began service in 1873, are now national historic landmarks. Their peak speed of up to nine and one-half miles an hour seems fast when the grade of the hill is 21 percent.

△ The Hyde Street Pier on San Francisco's Fisherman's Wharf, is a place where real working boats dock and go fishing every day.
▷ The Columbus Tower, built in 1905, was one of the few buildings in North Beach to survive the 1906 San Francisco earthquake. Its architecture contrasts with the Transamerica Pyramid, built in 1972.

△ Most prominent of California red wine grape varieties are Zinfandel and Cabernet Sauvignon, shown ready for harvest at St. Helena, a nineteenth-century town rich with the memorabilia of Robert Louis Stevenson who honeymooned there in 1880. ▷ After harvest, rows of grapevines stand like memorial crosses at Beringer Winery, one of 185 vintners in Napa Valley.

△ Called Fort Sutter when it was founded in 1848, Sacramento was established as the capital of California in 1854, just four years after the new state was admitted to the Union. In 1850, Sacramento showed a population of 6,820; figures for 1990 showed nearly 370,000. ▷ The Capitol, where the legislature still meets, was constructed in the Classical style between 1860 and 1869.

◁ The seathrift, or *Armeria maritima,* clings to a foothold just out of the splash zone on Salt Point in Salt Point State Park in Sonoma County. △ In 1812, a crew of Russians and Aleut Indians built a village and fort at Rossiya, now Fort Ross State Historical Park, only one hundred miles north of San Francisco. They came to hunt sea otter, grow food, and establish trade with the Mexican landowners.

△ With its numerous large, rounded rocks, Bowling Ball Beach seems well named. These sandstone concretions lie along the coast between Manchester and Point Arena in Mendocino State Park.

△ The town of Mendocino was founded in 1852 when San Franciscans came to the Mendocino coast and established the first successful sawmill in the area. The redwood lumber culled from the region helped build, and—after the 1906 earthquake—rebuild, San Francisco. ▷▷ A dormant volcano, Mount Shasta is a part of the Cascade Range, rising to a height of 14,162 feet.

△ Among the splendors that are visible on the two-hundred-mile loop between Mount Shasta and Lassen Peak is McArthur-Burney Falls—a favorite of Teddy Roosevelt. The falls drop 129 feet in a state park that is wrapped in trails. ▷ Lassen Peak, which rises to 10,457 feet, was an active volcano from 1914 to 1921.

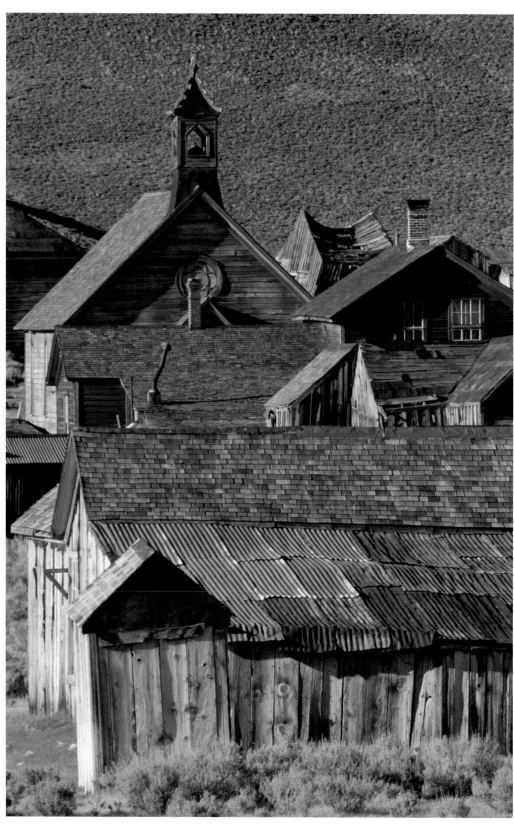

△ About 150 structures remain in a natural state of "arrested decay" at Bodie State Historical Park, thirty miles north of Tioga Pass. The town's population was twelve thousand in 1879. ▷ Twisted like giant bonzai, the amber trunks and limbs of bristlecone pines stab at the sky over the White Mountains. The oldest living bristlecone pine is forty-seven hundred years old.

△ Secluded glacial lakes fill pockets of the High Sierra at timberline. Some are surrounded entirely by rock—no marshes, no bushes, no beach. They mirror the jagged peaks above, tumbled boulders below. ▷ A state reserve and national forest scenic area protect much of Mono Lake. Fresh and saltwater combined to form the strange tufa sculptures.

△ Fields of blue lupine and other wildflowers brighten the foothills of the Gold Country as well as the higher trails and meadows of Yosemite National Park to the east. ▷ The sheer face of Half Dome is nearly a mile wide, and almost vertical. Carved by glaciers, it rises in bold glory forty-eight hundred feet above the floor of Yosemite Valley, which is four thousand feet above sea level.

◁ Below the High Sierra, the Alabama Hills have been the frequent setting for movie and TV Westerns. A plaque along Movie Road marks the area's Hollywood history. △ Sequoia and Kings Canyon National Parks shelter the world's largest living trees—the *Sequoia gigantea,* or giant sequoia. Though not as tall as coastal redwoods, sequoias have almost twice the girth.

△ A rosy dawn reveals the first snowfall of winter on the granite mass of Mount Whitney in the Sierra Nevada wall. At 14,494 feet, Whitney is the highest peak in the contiguous United States. America's low point, Death Valley, is only eighty miles east.